Designing KPIs to Drive Process Improvement

Giles Johnston

Copyright 2013 Giles Johnston

Disclaimer:

The author of this book has tried to present the most accurate information to his knowledge at the time of writing. This book is intended for information purposes only. The author does not imply any results to those using this book, nor is he responsible for any results brought about by the usage of the information contained herein.

Table of Contents

Introduction 5

Benefits of revising your existing KPIs 7

Analogy: KPIs are like a car's dashboard 9

Examples of KPI changes 11

Requirements to make the change 17

Principles to make KPI design easier 19

The process overview 21

Step 1 - Draw a KPI mapping chart 23

Step 2 - Main business process KPIs 27

Step 3 - Define the support department KPIs 31

Step 4 - Checks and balances 33

Step 5 - KPI checklist 35

Step 6 - Process improvements 37

Step 7 - Sanity check 41

Step 8 - Choose your targets 43

Step 9 - Use the information 47

Step 10 - KPI review meeting (agenda and example) 49

Maintain your focus 51

A quick word on 'standard' KPIs 55

Techniques to help the implementation 57

Make your KPIs even better 63

Final thoughts 65

Links and resources 67

About Giles Johnston 69

Introduction

Why do we need Key Performance Indicators?

Key Performance Indicators (KPIs) tell us about our performance. They can tell us how well we are doing as well as how well we have done. There is a difference.

Many businesses use KPIs but only the 'after the event' type. Once the month or the quarter has been completed they then know just how well they business has done, how much profit has been made and how well the business delivered on its orders. If something has gone wrong it is too late.

Other businesses include performance measures that tell them how well they are doing, this gives them the opportunity to 'shift gears' when it becomes obvious that their results won't meet their targets and what they are doing needs to change.

And there are other businesses that realise their process improvement projects will require a short term set of KPIs to drive the right kinds of behaviours in their business. These KPIs will feed into a higher set of business metrics, but serve a purpose to get the business on the right footing. Once the purpose has been met then the process improvement KPIs can be phased out and the focus shifted. Managing the higher level KPIs ensures that the right things are still being done, but the level of intervention can be less.

So, KPIs can serve a number of purposes within our business and although this short book will focus on designing KPIs that serve our process improvement needs we will also look at how the right KPIs can serve our business more effectively.

This book offers you a step by step process to follow and to help you determine what the right KPIs are for your business. We will touch on some of the standard KPI areas briefly for reference, but this book aims to help you determine a few key measures that will help your teams focus their attention on doing the right things at the right time so that you experience the change in business performance that you are looking for.

Benefits of revising your existing KPIs

Your business may well have KPIs in place as you read this.

As discussed in the last section, knowing exactly how you are doing at any point in time in your business is essential if you want to be sure that you are going to arrive at your chosen destination. Many businesses implement Key Performance Indicators but don't get the best out of them.

The choices made, to manage the business using these KPIs are then forgotten and the day to day activities are undertaken regardless. Years may pass before these businesses realise that their KPIs don't actually help them. There are many businesses that record the information but don't do anything constructive with it.

Measuring the wrong things can also be disastrous. Many organisations think they can tell you how well they are doing, but talking to their customers paints a different picture. Are we measuring what we can measure, or measuring the vital life signs of how our business operates?

We have the opportunity in this book to look at how we can define KPIs that are easy to maintain but quickly tell us exactly how well we are doing.

Why is it important to get your KPIs right?

- Your lead-times can reduce in your business because the right things happen at the right time meaning that your business processes become tighter and more organised.
- On time delivery performance can increase. If we keep correcting and using the KPI information to help us improve our business then we can get better and better at giving our customers what they want.
- There can be fewer surprises within the business. When information is buried within the business it can be a shock when it suddenly arrives in a management meeting and reveals itself. By knowing the information before we get to that position we can make the necessary corrections in our day to day activities.
- We can also define the necessary 'checks and balances' that can tell us if we are doing the right things at the right time. These might not be something that you need to report on, but if you recall the phenomenon of cause and effect; KPIs are the effects and what we do are the causes.

If running your business in a tighter, more controlled manner is going to help you then please read on.

Analogy: KPIs are like a car's dashboard

To help send the message home of how this book is going to approach designing KPIs then this short analogy should help clarify as well as give you an easy example to explain to your colleagues.

If you look at the dashboard of your car when you are driving you will see a panel full of dials and gauges. Each instrument can tell you one piece of the story about how your journey is going. In a few moments, by considering these various bits of information, you can quickly determine if your journey is going be successful.

The alternative option would be to not look at any information and then hope that when you get to your destination you are on time (and that you have used your fuel efficiently in the process, or whatever else is important to you).

We wouldn't take the second option. We would periodically check the instruments to make sure that we were on track. We would consider our speed and our engine revs to ensure we are being efficient with our fuel. We would compare our trip counter against our clock to work out if we were going to arrive on time. We would look at our temperature gauges and satisfy ourselves that our driving was going to be successful. And of course we would check the fuel gauge from time to time - just to make sure!

When we look at businesses many of them are measuring themselves at the finish line.
They ask themselves 'how did we do?'
If this makes little sense from the viewpoint of driving a car, why does it make sense in our businesses? You have the opportunity to determine some useful and easy to maintain KPIs, measures that will help you steer your business in the right direction at the right times.
You won't have to worry about arriving late; you will know how you are doing long before you arrive.

Examples of KPI changes

To help put the idea of having a range of KPIs (outcome, process and improvement) into context, here are some examples of how other business have used their measures.

'Late at workcentre'

A manufacturing business had trouble with achieving their on-time delivery dates. Upon investigation it turned out that the work did not start on time, with each production cell becoming progressively more behind schedule. To compliment their existing KPIs we introduced 'late at work centre' as a process measure.

'Late at work centre' allowed us to see how the orders kept to schedule, and in particular if they started the entire process on-time. By focusing on this KPI for a period of time the approach to running the production area changed and the systems that supported the area also changed. After a period of approximately 3 months this KPI was looked at on a weekly basis (it had originally been daily) as the production process was now under control from a scheduling perspective.

The on time delivery measure followed suit and this (with a

handful of other measures including unit costs and profit per person) was used to ensure that the business was working as planned.

'Planning activity'

A retailing business had already implemented a range of KPIs when we got involved on a lead-time reduction project for them (a lead time is the time between two points in a process. In most cases this is how long it takes for an order to be placed with your business until the product leaves your premises or until your services are delivered).

Their KPIs were quite comprehensive already, but did not include any 'checks and balances'. Simply put - they weren't running their planning function, but they were measuring the outputs of a system that wasn't being managed properly!

We determined all the things that should be happening from a management perspective and then started to report on these weekly. This is like a public declaration of a checklist, but it works well.

Over a period of a few days the day to day tasks were starting to be adhered to, this became obvious from the stability of the day to day operations, there was significantly less fire fighting. Less mistakes (or omissions) led to better planning and ultimately that allowed the business to shrink their lead times. The output measure reflected this and the business started to achieve its objectives.

'The Magic Number'

A manufacturing business had trouble focussing their efforts onto the orders that needed to be processed next, there was a lot of interference in the business caused by a lack of focus and people perpetually chased their tails trying to get the job done. Once we reviewed a very top level map of the business process it was clear that we needed to change one part of the scheduling process and the focus of the team leaders. The team leaders came up with the name of the 'magic number', a reference to the size of the queue at a bottleneck process.

Every day at 3pm the magic number was reviewed, its change from the previous day was recorded and the direction of travel. After two weeks this figure was only 20% of its original total. Focus was applied to one specific area without the need to re-engineer the process, and as the meetings continued the team came up with ways to improve the scheduling of the bottleneck so that it had minimal impact on the overall schedule.

'Capacity Planning'

A government organisation was delivering a service in the community that had a variable demand. The service was set up in a rigid fashion; their team would be available on specific days and times in specific areas of the community. Overloads were never managed - they were left, with the service users hoping to be at the front of the queue next time.

However, from reviewing the process at a top level, it was clear that there was some form of demand information being passed on to the organisation – people were booking appointments. There was a disconnection in the process. The timetable of service delivery had been defined at a point in time when the demand profile was more stable.

Our simple approach was to develop some delivery scenarios – alternative timetables depending on the changing demand which could be put in place quickly depending on the demand being received via the bookings. This meant that the service could be delivered in different areas for different periods of time, efficiently, by using some existing information in the organisation.

KPIs can make a huge difference to the performance of a process and I hope by the end of this book you will be able to find some measures that you can get behind and really use to make a difference to your business.

Requirements to make the change

To get the best out of this book I suggest that you do the following:

Read this book at least once on your own to familiarise yourself with the approach and the main steps. By understanding the steps and the process that you are about to go through you will be better prepared when it comes to running the exercise.

Gather a team of people who can reflect on the different steps you have in your business. By getting various points of view on this exercise you will be creating a better solution for your business. The more information you have about a subject the better the decisions that you can make about it. Whilst we don't want you to get into a 'management by committee' situation about this exercise, doing it alone is never as good as doing it with a handful of other people.

Then, get the team of people together and take them through this process. Keep the session light, keep it fun and keep it focussed on making your business improve. The steps of the process are designed so that people can get involved with the activity, and then work out what they have just done afterward. The session should be mainly focussed on sharing ideas and insights. Evaluating the ideas during the main activity sometimes dampens down the enthusiasm of the team.

You may also need to make plenty of blank paper / flipcharts available so that ideas can be recorded. Encouragement of any ideas should be welcomed.

If you have a team that have issues with the business generally then it may be a good idea to vent these at the start of the workshop session, before you get into the steps outlined in the following pages. Write them down, discuss them briefly and then agree not to discuss them again. If people wander back onto their 'chosen subjects' then you can politely remind them of their previous agreement!

Once you have completed the exercises in this book it is then time to make some decisions about how you want to improve your business. It is at this point that we must take our observations and insights from doing this exercise and put them into action.

Principles to make KPI design easier

Measure the process not just the outcome

Waiting for the final result in order to work out whether or not you have done a good job is not always a great plan. In most circumstances this is usually a poor approach. If we can work out what results we are creating as we are in the process of creating them then we can do something different if required. If you changed your mind about the destination of a day trip you wouldn't drive there and then go somewhere else if you knew before hand - would you?

Make KPIs meaningful

The clue is in the title - KEY Performance Indicators. Each business has its own way of conducting business, so it has its own little quirks, advantages and disadvantages. Make the KPIs meaningful to you and your business. Yes, there are some KPIs which are fairly generic that you can apply, but get creative and think about what pieces of information your business would really benefit from so that you can exploit your inherent advantages.

Spread ownership

Don't make KPIs the sole responsibility of one team or person. Each person who runs a part of the business should have something they can report on. Find out who and what this agreement needs to be and put it in place.

Use the information

Many times businesses don't actually use the KPI information to help them improve the business, at least on a continuous basis. If you are going to revise / implement your key performance indicators then make sure that you are committed to using them properly. KPIs should be there to guide your decisions, not just for a short term fix.

The process overview

Over the next few pages you are going to be following a series of steps, these are:

- Drawing a KPI mapping chart

- Filling in the chart - main business process

- Filling in the chart - supporting departments

- Defining checks and balances

- KPI checklist

- Identifying specific process improvements and their KPIs

- Doing a sanity check - preventing KPI overload!

- Setting targets

- Using the information

Step 1 - Draw a KPI mapping chart

Our first step is to draw a chart to help with the brainstorming of the KPIs.

We are going to follow the SIPOC structure for doing this. SIPOC stands for:

- Suppliers

- Inputs

- Process

- Outputs

- Customers

By using these headings and then generating potential measures you will be covering the entire scope of activity through your business. A blank mapping chart can be found at the end of this section for you to use with your team.

The key to this chart is that we need to be able to define what each part of the process needs to tell us. This process can be anything you choose it to be, but for the first time following this exercise we would recommend that you follow the order fulfilment process that generates income for the business. This should be the process that is used to turn enquiries into products / services and then invoices.

The supporting parts of the mapping chart are there to cover the KPIs required for the rest of the business. These other areas are there to support - so we need to know how well they are doing in terms of delivering their support.

KPI Mapping Chart

	Suppliers	Inputs	Processes	Outputs	Customers
Human Resources					
Sales and Marketing					
IT					
Finance					

Step 2 - Main business process KPIs

Now that we have a framework to use it is time to come up with some ideas about KPIs.

If you have existing KPIs it is worth noting these on the chart.

The stages on the sheet are to prompt your thinking about what KPIs would help.

The stages are:

Suppliers - what tells us if the people / businesses that are feeding our system are doing the right things?

Inputs - how do we know if what we are putting into our business process is correct?

Process - what do we need to know to make sure our customers get what they want when they want it?

Outputs – did we meet our delivery schedule / promised delivery date? Did we achieve our unit costs of production?

Customers - Is our delivered product or service achieving the specification that the customer requested? Are they happy?

Review your business against these key stages and write down whatever comes to mind that can tell you the above. You may want to break the process stage down into the key steps within that process.

To help you get started some examples when generating ideas could include:

Suppliers:

- On-time supply of materials or services
- Defects per order
- Delivery lead-time from receipt of your purchase order

Inputs:

- Variations from the customer (changes to their original request)
- % of 'dirty orders' – orders that are incomplete upon first arrival
- planning horizon available from the customer (how much visibility of orders you have)

Process:

- On-time by department (on time start or on time finish)
- Process lead-time
- Yield of processes
- Utilisation of equipment
- Unit costs of operating the process

Output:

- On-time in full (OTIF) delivery performance
- Delivery Schedule Adherence
- Profit per order / person
- Shipping costs as a percentage of overall costs

Customer:

- Satisfaction ratings
- Warranty claims value

There are also some additional boxes on the SIPOC chart for use with the next step, the supporting departments.

Step 3 - Define the support department KPIs

The next step is to consider which other areas of the business support this main 'process' running through your business.

For example HR may exist with the purpose of 'training staff to be exceptional at their job' and you may choose to develop measurements that reflect the amount and level of training offered to staff. You may also wish to measure staff turnover and sick days per year. All of these factors help to tell a story about how your business is doing.

Which support departments do you have, and what KPIs could help you work out if they are helping the business achieve its objectives?

The mapping chart also includes some of these other functions for you to consider.

The purpose of this approach is to define support department metrics that can tell you how they are doing with respect to your main process. An example of a completed KPI chart is on the next page.

KPI Mapping Chart - Example

Suppliers	Inputs	Processes	Outputs	Customers
On time delivery	Order changes	Internal on time delivery	OTIF	Satisfaction
Quality	Dirty orders	Cycle times	DSA	Warranty claims
Lead times	Horizon available	Utilisation	Profit	
		Yield	Shipping costs	
Human Resources – Hours of training per person per month			
Sales and Marketing – Number of issues with customer orders older than one week			
IT – Uptime for servers / Number of issues older than two days			
Finance – Number of suppliers on 'stop'			

Step 4 - Checks and balances

The KPIs that have been identified in steps two and three above are likely to be quantitative in their nature, providing a percentage figure or numerical answer as their results. These measures are likely to be the outcomes of the activities taking place. What about the causes of these effects?

It is quite possible to add some simple 'yes / no' checks into the mix that can be reported on to help tell you if the process is being managed correctly..

For example, if you are managing a production process then every week you may measure the lead-time, the yield of the process and the on-time delivery to the next stage. These are all measurable in numerical terms.

If you also take into account that an achievable production schedule was updated and available at the start of each week then you may have more confidence about achieving your schedule. This single 'yes/no' check could tell you before you set off for the week's production if you were likely to succeed. Although this is an example, I see many real life instances of people running processes that haven't been started correctly, you can guess what results they achieve on that basis!

Would you want to run a process that isn't initiated correctly?

The main benefit of including this type of information in the KPI mix is that it tells you if your system is working the way it was designed, or not.

One of the hardest things to do is keep a system running; many times people wander off course and do things their own way.

Keeping an eye on the critical events that need to keep happening (such as the creation of a production schedule) can help you achieve great performance within your business.

Combining 'checks and balances' with relevant KPIs can give you a 'closed loop' feedback system that can really help you to make improvements on an ongoing basis.

In my experience, adding in a few 'checks and balances' can make one of the biggest jumps in performance if the discipline and habits of your teams aren't as strong as you would like.

So, what checks and balances do you want to use in your business?

Step 5 - KPI checklist

We have reviewed three specific areas for selecting KPIs for our business; the main process, the supporting departments and checks and balances. To help you with your thinking here are some questions that you may want to consider as you review your list:

- Do your KPIs cover the entirety of your business and its processes?

- Can you review your Quality, your Costs and your Delivery performance with these KPIs?

- Is your information correct, complete and without gaps?

- Do you have the means to gather and analyse the information to create the KPIs?

- Do you have time during the day / week / month to gather and analyse the information?

- Do you have the discipline present in your business to maintain this system of measurement?

- Will you define points in the week / month / year to review your KPIs so that you can determine if you are doing the right things at the right time?

- Have you included 'cause' KPIs (yes / no) to ensure our day to day working is effective?

- Have you integrated the KPIs into your day to day working practices?

- Will the KPIs chosen drive the correct behaviours and not compromise quality?

Step 6 - Process improvements

When you have a change project taking place in the business on top of the general need to improve the performance of the existing processes you need to think slightly differently about KPIs. Whereas KPIs are normally used to provide focus and gauge performance so that corrective action can be undertaken, sometimes we need to overhaul the measurement method we use with the process entirely. When we are in this position then there is the possibility of using short term KPIs to help with both the implementation of the change as well as the embedding of the change itself.

Creating implementation KPIs might be appropriate when you have a high volume of work to undertake in order to effect the change. If this is the case then you can set targets for daily achievements and measure these during the implementation phase. These types of measures often work best when there is a risk that the day to day tasks get in the way of making the improvement project tasks happen. Once the change has been made the measures are redundant and can be ignored, but it will serve a purpose for getting the change made.

For embedding the change you may want to consider measuring smaller, specific parts of the process. In particular the 'yes / no' measures we discussed in step 4 might be appropriate, especially when you are trying to form new habits. Measuring the details and habits are easier to do when a process is new or changing and more difficult later on. When the process change is establishing itself as the new normal way of working (as opposed to just being documented!) you can relax the KPIs accordingly. The higher level KPIs should be able to take the strain of giving you the right information once the process is working the way it was designed.

One of the really useful things to do when you are changing how a process works in order to achieve a higher level of performance is to make sure you have used your KPIs to give you your starting position. What do your KPIs say to you prior to the start of the process change? This is certainly one of the objective ways that you will be able to determine whether the process changes are being effective or not, as well as how quickly the change is happening.

Once you have your improvement plan (as often the KPIs can inform you as to what needs changed and how) you can define targets for the implementation that link into key stages of the improvement projects. The combination of milestones in your improvement project plan and the corresponding KPIs should give you some really good management tools to help you determine if you are on the right tracks or whether you need to modify your approach to the process improvement.

So, KPIs can be used for local, specific, projects where a finer level of detail is required. They can also be used to help with both the implementation by measuring the progress of the actions as well as being used to help form the right habits to make the process robust longer term.

Next, we'll get back to our overall list of KPIs for our business and start pulling them together so that we can use them to improve our business' performance.

Step 7 - Sanity check

Once you have all of your KPIs defined it is a good idea to step back and let the list settle for a little while. When you come back to your list it is worthwhile considering how valid this list still is. If you have been a little too ambitious then the list of KPIs may be too long to be manageable. If you deduce that the time required to compile and analyse would be better spent on managing the process then reducing the list and removing the less essential KPIs is a good idea.

The perception of the KPIs is another perspective to consider. If there is a risk that they will be perceived as oppressive or them being 'measures for the sake of measuring', then it is worth evaluating their necessity or the communication given out to the teams affected by the KPIs as to your intention with the information.

And of course, you may have realised that you have missed a couple of key areas that do need to be measured. If you think through how the business works you might want to ask yourself 'do these KPIs and checks support my business to become even better?'

Hopefully, after reading the above, you will not have to change your list too much. Even better I hope that you have some form of business information system (such as MRP / ERP) that can allow you to pull the data out of the system at the touch of the button. Having the KPI data (semi-)automated makes life easier all round, means it can be reported at any point in time and is a little harder for people to interfere with should they want to skew the results.

Considering the robustness of the information is a valid point. If you are basing your decisions on the KPIs suite you are developing you need to ensure that the inputs to your figures / calculations will stand up to scrutiny. I have seen many businesses that are running their operations based on information that is not correct. I am not just talking about people being malicious with the information, but data that is not maintained or not understood and then being used to make decisions with, that move the business in the wrong direction.

By now you should be looking at a revised list of KPIs (with the least amount of manual input) which you are confident provide the right information, and can be relied upon for decision making at the highest levels of your business.

Step 8 - Choose your targets

To be effective KPIs need context. Measuring on time delivery rates, for example, but not knowing what is good from a customer point of view is meaningless (100% is good in this particular case). Some customers will tell you what they expect, in the form of a Service Level Agreement (SLA) or similar.

So the next step is to work out what a good KPI result is. To get to your good result it might be necessary to pick something a little easier and work towards that before raising the bar and moving to where you actually want to be. The people who are doing the work to achieve the KPI results may need to be coaxed and staging the targets is a good technique to do this.

For example, let's say that you want to reduce your lead time for delivering a product. If our target is going to be eight days and we are currently at twenty two days we may set the targets as:

1st target = 18 days
2nd target = 15 days
3rd target = 12 days
4th target = 10 days

5th target = 8 days

However you do need to keep working towards excellence. There is no end to this process, you keep on choosing a new target to aim for and see what you can do to make the improvements.

An additional point I would like to make here is that the direction of travel is also important to note. We will touch again on this point in a moment, but some days (or weeks / months) when you take a measurement it will be worse than it was the last time. The direction of travel can tell us if we are still heading in the right direction, levelling off, or getting worse. It is natural (and frustrating) to see our KPIs head in the wrong direction, but we need to be clear whether we are witnessing a blip or a full blow change of direction. Taking the current and last two results (three in total) should give you a better picture of whether you really are heading towards your targets or not.

Going back to the splitting up of targets into smaller jumps is often something that managers read or hear about and then ignore. I'm fairly certain that in most cases they need to jump to the finish line as that is what they are going to get measured against. The reason for splitting the KPI target down into steps is to do with the people who are involved with the work to achieve the target. Making a large jump can put a lot of people off doing the work in the first place. I don't want this to sound like we just want to be nice because they are a little intimidated with the performance change, but if they haven't achieved this level of performance before and need to play a part in achieving the new target, then tiny steps can make a big difference to the rate of change you experience. You can often be very surprised how quickly people can achieve the new targets if provided with a structured approach. A big jump can seem too far removed from where they are now, but the next small step can appear doable. This approach allows you to build momentum, as well as getting started in the first place.

Step 9 - Use the information

Now that you have a wealth of information it is time to do something with it.

How many times have you seen a business that records and reports management information, but no one seems to act on this guidance?

I have seen many businesses that diligently record the information and convert it into graphs and charts but don't then use it to make any changes to the way that the business operates. Remember, KPIs provide focus, and changing your focus can change your results. Please don't let your business be another casualty; make the information work for you so you can achieve the results you want to achieve.

Decide when in the week or the month (or the day) you will review the information. By doing this on a consistent basis you will be able to spot the trends in what is happening and make some changes to how your business works.

My last job as an Operations Manager started every morning with my KPIs. Specifically I knew the number of jobs 'stuck' in our production system, and importantly where they were stuck. Each department had a score and if it wasn't 'zero jobs stuck' then I would start my day by visiting them. This change in behaviour allowed my teams to reach on time delivery rates in excess of 95% consistently (peaking at 98%) in just three months. Quite a significant jump from 22%! This was my routine and it got results. The right focus with the right information and having the right conversations is often where results are to be found.

For some KPIs you may want to have a specific meeting to help with either the change projects, or the general management of the process to achieve the performance objectives. I have included an example agenda for such a review meeting (see next section). Please amend and modify this format to suit your business' needs and use it accordingly. Like all business improvement approaches - if you get involved with the improvement activity in your business then you will find a better way to do it. You will find a better way that suits your working environment and ultimately you will find a way to do it that suits your way of working.

Also, if you find your team is getting stuck with their improvement projects / achieving the process' performance generally then please note that there are some ideas to help them make progress that we will discuss in a few pages time.

Step 10 - KPI review meeting (agenda and example)

- What are the KPI figures?

- How do they compare against their targets?

- What is the direction of travel? [Last three results for comparison.]

- Why did this variation occur? [This is a good opportunity to do some root cause analysis and improve the system.]

- Checks and balances - did all of our routine tasks happen on-time?

- Agree actions based on above points.

- Close meeting.

e.g. KPI - On Time Delivery

Actual - 78%

Target - 85%

Direction of travel – still upward towards target (not at rate desired)

Notes / Root Cause – Paperwork missing, late start of jobs

Checks and Balances – Not all admin routines are being followed

Actions – Instruct Office Manager to reinforce routines and refocus Production Manager on the 'on time start' requirements

e.g. KPI - Internal production lead time

Actual - 8 days

Target - 3 days

Direction of travel - static

Notes / Root Cause - handing over of information packs requires re-work

Check and Balances – daily production meeting happening, but check regarding shop floor paperwork not being asked

Actions – Move shop floor paperwork check to top of agenda for the next week.

Maintain your focus

I hope by now that you have picked up that this book is all about using appropriate KPIs to help you focus on the right things to improve in your business. Developing business processes using KPIs only works when you keep your focus on what you are trying to improve. There is a saying 'what you focus on becomes your reality'. I don't recall where I first heard that phrase but I have heard variations of it over the years. If you keep focussing on achieving your business' targets for performance then you are much more likely to think about it more often, come up with more ideas and be more likely to persist where others would give up.

We have discussed setting targets. In most businesses the owners, or senior management, set the targets for you. There will possibly, however, come a time when you achieve their targets and start setting your own. You get to define the standards that will shape the ongoing development and improvement of the processes you manage. I have done this myself and know many others who have done the same. They have set higher targets than their managers have set. I did it because I wanted the business I worked for to be the best in its sector. I'm sure others have their own reasons for wanting to set higher than required targets.

When you are improving a process then it is vital that you keep the focus, and pressure, on the process until it has achieved the result wanted. We need to make our improvement targets important within the business so people don't just pass off this improvement project as another one that will fail and await its collapse. We need the people involved to realise that it is important. When the process has been improved and it has achieved its performance target and has proven itself to be stable (plus it has been documented with Standard Operating Procedures and the team trained etc...) then you can shift your focus. Of course you can never fully let go, but the intensity of the focus can lessen.

If you have daily (or weekly or monthly) management reviews then build the KPIs into the agenda. Make them a central piece to your management meetings and give them the proper place that they deserve in your business. The KPIs will relate to something important and so they are a good way to start off a management review. The necessary discussions that follow and the actions that get agreed to should have an effect on the KPIs so make reviewing your measures part of the way you and your team work.

Reviewing KPIs can have a really good effect on production when the information is shared with the teams responsible for achieving the targets. Whether production for you means the factory floor, the construction site, the admin office or something else, knowing how you are doing and having a context to set this in can really help with focussing minds. If you put this against your (next) performance target then it can really help to make the importance of process improvement clear to everyone.

If you are responsible for a team then try making KPIs the start of your working day. Direct your focus on the few things that will make most of the difference and use this management information to help guide your thoughts and actions so that you can make the biggest impact during your working day.

Finally, as touched upon above, never let go of a KPI once your focus has changed to another area for improvement. Build the KPIs into an efficient routine so that you can remain abreast of the way your business is operating. Using KPIs is a habit and, like any other effective habit you need to develop it to manage and lead your business and reap the rewards of doing so.

A quick word on 'standard' KPIs

I'm guessing the reason that you bought this book was that you didn't want a standard list of KPIs that you could apply into your business. You wanted to develop a suite of measures that would tell you something about how *your* business operates, something that you can use to identify improvements.

However, I feel it is worth touching upon some of the standard KPIs that are mentioned in business, for a degree of completeness for this book.

One of the best 'standard' lists is that produced by the (then) Department of Trade and Industry in the UK. You can find the list online by using a search engine where you can find the details of the calculations if you want more information. The list includes:

- Not right first time
- Delivery schedule adherence
- People productivity
- Stock turns
- Overall equipment effectiveness (aka, OEE)
- Value added per person

- Floor space utilisation

All of these KPIs are useful, but some more than others. Some will be used periodically and some regularly. The intention of this book was to help you create a range of KPIs that will help you to drive the performance of a process, so look into the measures above on the Internet if you think they will add value to your existing suite.

If the focus of this book had been about stock management, strategic decision making or manufacturing throughput then the list above would have a different significance.

So, do your homework and incorporate these measures if appropriate.

Techniques to help the implementation

I realise that reading a book and doing the work required to gain the benefits are two different things. This section offers some ideas should you find yourself (and your team) getting stuck when it comes to implementing effective KPIs.

Too many KPIs

One of the problems that I hear often, and one that we touched upon earlier, is having too many KPIs to manage in your business. If you feel that this is affecting you, group the KPIs together depending on what kind of information they offer / what area they represent and then try to rationalise based on how useful the information is. Quite often we reproduce information and give it a new name when really we should become more familiar with our existing KPIs. I see this quite often when people don't use their existing KPIs and create new ones to compensate. So, group and trim.

Not making progress towards a target

A lack of progress toward a target can be de-motivating for your team and using smaller increments of targets can often be a way to get things moving. Rather than just relaxing the target, you can engage in a conversation with your team to plan out the journey to the next target, but use smaller increments to facilitate the planning. Checking off the smaller targets on the way to your next target is then just a means to an end to achieving the result. The size of a challenge is always an interesting discussion. How big is big? Whilst this is a long conversation (with no end) going the other way and agreeing on what is small is easier. You can usually break down targets, or tasks, into their smallest component and the reason for doing this is to prevent the people involved from getting worried about not being able to complete the task. This modern day manifestation of the 'fight or flight' response can play havoc but small targets can take the problem away.

Not maintaining the information

If you are experiencing unreliable KPIs because of poor data then it is time to find out where the data is coming from.

Many times the data is bad because the person who puts it into the system either doesn't understand the requirements of the data entry (or has done it incorrectly) or is behind on their work and haven't done it. If they haven't done the work in the first place then reviewing their routines / workloads is a good place to start. If the information is important then the data entry needs to be done.

If the work is inadequate then developing some form of housekeeping process, or tool, is a good option to take. If your data is coming out of a central computer system (again, MRP / ERP / MIS / CRM etc...) then you should be able to create a basic report that checks that the data entries are complete and in the right format. The corrections required can then be fed back to the person responsible for updating that part of the system allowing us to close the loop of bad data.

Not realising tangible benefits

When you have been working on improving a process for a while you should be able to see some kind of tangible benefit in the business. Sometimes this isn't as obvious as you would hope. Sometimes the improvement you are working on is a means to an end and it will enable you to do something else that would give you a tangible benefit.

For example, let's say that you are measuring your production throughput and you are focussing on increasing the throughput to give you a reduction in unit costs and the ability to cope with variable demands. And let's say that you have noticed an increase in throughput but the unit cost hasn't come down to the level you had hoped for. And then let us say that we had been running overtime in the factory to achieve our previous output. If we don't decrease our overtime then we can't realise our target unit costs (and we will possibly face an overproduction situation). The increase throughput allows us to reduce overtime (or sub-contracting or whatever) and is therefore a means to an end.

Being clear on what effect different performances will have on the business is essential if we are to understand what kind of tangible benefit will be gained.

Lack of buy in with senior management

The final difficulty that we will look at is when the people above you in your organisation don't respond to the KPIs. Perhaps they don't support you in the way that you had hoped for, or perhaps they don't see the value in what you are recording.

Assuming that the KPIs are worth investing time and effort into and that they will help your business drive up its performance there could be the issue of perception once more. If your superiors don't understand what the KPIs are telling them then they run the risk of being dismissed (rather than you being told that they don't understand them). The common language of most senior people in businesses is money. Converting your KPIs into a monetary figure may be the only way to get them involved in the discussion. For best usage the KPI may need to be represented as both the original value (figure, percentage, ratio etc...) as well as the monetary value.

I hope these four ideas help you with your implementation and usage of KPIs in your business.

Make your KPIs even better

KPIs sometimes have a shelf life. What is relevant today might not be relevant in the future. It is entirely feasible that KPIs might be created from this exercise because certain processes are not under control, as we discussed in Step 5.

As time passes and as improved systems of control are implemented then measuring these particular 'out of control' processes may become less relevant.

Keep what is working and change the rest.

You could also look at how you would run this exercise again when you do come to review the KPIs.

How we created the KPIs today may not be the way that you want to do it next time. As you and your team have gone through this process you will have possibly learnt a different approach. Changing the people who are involved with the KPI design process, reviewing different functions and changing the focus of where the business is going to can change the way the KPIs are identified.

Get feedback from your team about the process described in this book and find out what they would do differently. The process detailed in this book is effective, but it has been created by years of experience and client interaction through Smartspeed. It is our process. Give your team the chance to make it theirs. If you do, and if they tweak it to suit them, then you will have a sustainable tool for future use.

Final thoughts

Great Key Performance Indicators can help you make great business decisions. If you get them right they can tell you what you need to know in order to maximise the performance of your business. A lot of people minimise their work issues, saying that things are going well when in fact they aren't. KPIs help to get past these comments. They help to draw a picture that can put the reality into context.

This of course means that you will need to keep up the KPIs, keeping their data up to date so that they can be relied upon. It is an unappealing sight when you view a KPI board only to see out of date information - now what does that tell you about the organisation?

Following on from this is the fact that standards shouldn't slip. Deciding that you are going to report on KPIs and then stopping sends the wrong message back into the business, so make sure that your KPI choices are easy to maintain and are built into your management routines so that this situation is less likely to occur. Decaying standards in one area of a business have a tendency to migrate to other areas of the business so beware.

If the performance of the business doesn't improve under the set of KPIs you have chosen then please review the advice provided earlier on. If there are specific areas that need support then you can consider reviewing Step 5 again and validating that what you are measuring and focussing upon will give you the results you are looking for. If not, it would be worthwhile going through the steps once more.

KPIs should provide a lot of opportunities for meaningful conversations. I find that most change happens within a business when two (or more) people come together, share some ideas and the 'penny drops' for one or more of the people in the conversation. Change comes from insights, which can come from reviewing your KPIs. This in turn can provide the information to focus your conversations on the right parts of your business process.

So, KPIs should not be seen as an administrative burden but as an efficient tool to help you focus on specific areas of your business to drive process improvement.

Good luck with your improvements.

Giles

Links and resources

Free On Time Delivery Guide

If you want some ideas around improving the on time delivery performance of your business, then please download my free guide. You will need to register your email address on my website, the link is:

http://www.systemsandprocesses.co.uk

LinkedIn OTIF Forum

If you would like to join me and others online to discuss practical ideas around improving on time delivery performance then please visit our LinkedIn group:

http://www.linkedin.com/groups/On-Time-Delivery-Improvement-4419220/about

'Making It Happen' online course

Discover practical change management strategies with my online course, aimed at accelerating the rate of change at your place of work.

www.systemsandprocesses.co.uk/making-it-happen-lean-tools/

About Giles Johnston

Giles is a Chartered Engineer with a background in Operations Management. He spends most of his time working on capacity planning and 'on time delivery' improvement projects.

Giles has worked in a variety of different roles within manufacturing and as a consultant for a prestigious university.

In 2005 Giles decided to forge his own path and created Smartspeed, which has been helping businesses to improve their delivery performance, along with their profits, ever since.

Giles can be contacted by:

Email - gilesjohnston@smartspeed.co.uk

Website - www.smartspeed.co.uk

Printed in Great Britain
by Amazon